TO:

FROM:

DATE:

First published by Christian Art Publishers
PO Box 1599, Vereeniging, 1930, RSA
This edition published under licence.

This edition published by Monarch Books
an imprint of
Lion Hudson plc
Wilkinson House, Jordan Hill Road,
Oxford OX2 8DR, England
Email: monarch@lionhudson.com
www.lionhudson.com/monarch

ISBN 978 0 85721 762 2

First edition 2015
This edition 2016

Acknowledgments
Images used under licence from Shutterstock.com
Cover designed by Lion Hudson

A catalogue record for this book is available from the British Library

Printed and bound in Slovenia, February 2016, LH48

Shine

Colour your life beautiful

Colouring therapy with Scripture verses

MONARCH
BOOKS

Oxford, UK, and Grand Rapids, USA

WE HAVE THIS
HOPE
AS AN ANCHOR FOR THE SOUL.
HEBREWS 6:19

Rejoice
IN THE
LORD.
PHILIPPIANS 4:4

God
grant me
the
serenity
to accept
the things
I cannot change;
courage to
change
the things
I CAN;
& wisdom
to know the
difference.

THE
Whole earth
IS FILLED WITH AWE AT YOUR
WONDERS.
Psalm 65:8

If I settle on the
far side
of the SEA,
even there
Your hand
will
GUIDE
me.
Psalm 139:9-10

LET THE
SEA & everything in it
shout
HIS praise!
Psalm 98:7

Praise
the Lord from the EARTH,
you creatures
of
the OCEAN
depths.
Psalm 148:7

LET YOUR
light
Shine
BEFORE
OTHERS.
MATTHEW 5:16

Don't tell
GOD
HOW
Big your
storm is.
Tell the storm
HOW Big your
GOD is!

In high tide or low tide
God will be by your side.

TRUST
in the
LORD
with all your
HEART
PROVERBS 3:5

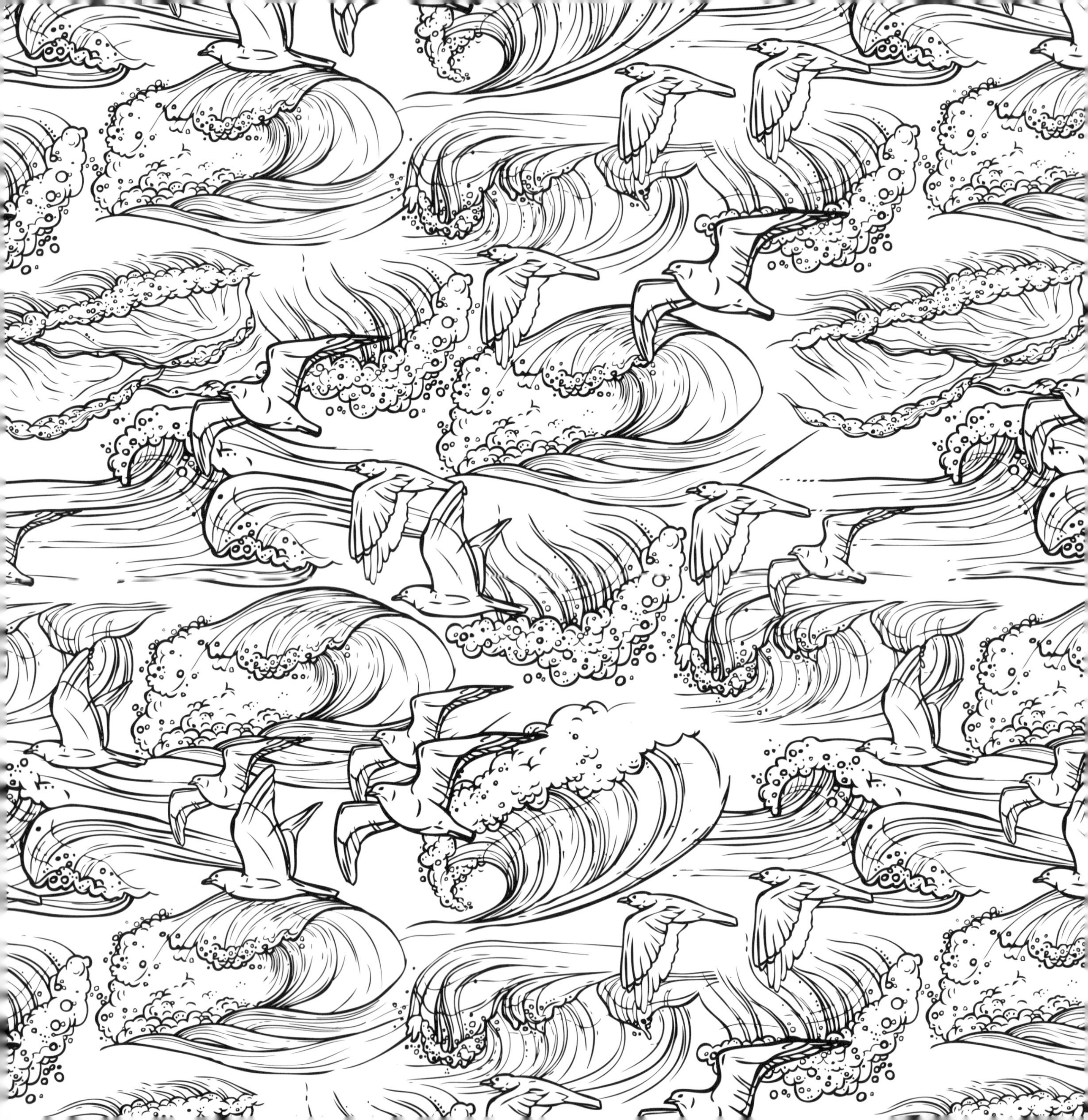

When You Go
THROUGH
DEEP
WATERS,
I will be
WITH
You.
ISAIAH 43:2

THE LORD
RESTORES
MY
SOUL.
PSALM 23:3

OH, GIVE
THANKS
TO THE LORD!
1 CHRONICLES 16:8

Hope
IN
THE
Lord
Psalm 130:7

LET
HEAVEN & EARTH
PRAISE
Him
Psalm 69:34

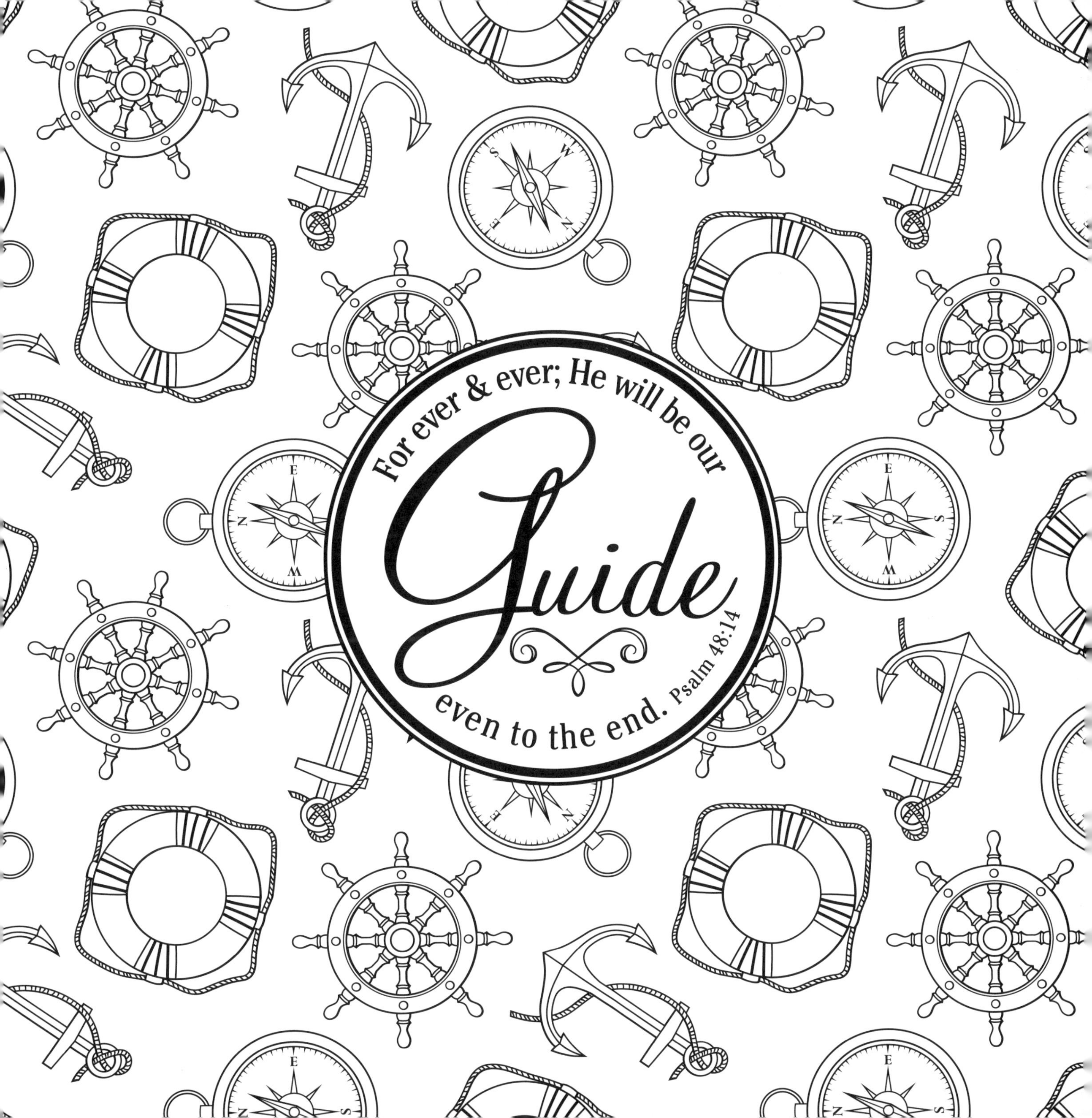
For ever & ever; He will be our
Guide
even to the end.
Psalm 48:14

HE WHO DWELLS IN THE SHELTER OF THE MOST High
WILL rest IN THE SHADOW OF THE ALMIGHTY
PSALM 91:1

Amazing
Grace
how sweet
the Sound
that
Saved
a
Wretch
Like Me

Sea
Sea
Sea
Sea

THE
LORD
IS MY
LIGHT
MICAH 7:8

PSALM 93:4
MIGHTIER THAN
THE THUNDER
OF THE
GREAT WATERS
MIGHTIER THAN
THE BREAKERS
OF THE SEA -
THE LORD ON HIGH
IS MIGHTY.

More than the grains of sand are His thoughts for you!

THE EARTH shall be filled with the
KNOWLEDGE of the
GLORY of the LORD
as the WATERS cover the
SEA.
HABAKKUK 2:14

BE STILL
AND
KNOW THAT I AM
GOD
PSALM 46:10

SING
TO THE
LORD
A PSALM OF PRAISE.
PSALM 47:7

BE JOYFUL
IN HOPE.
Romans 12:12

Jesus
IS THE
LIGHTHOUSE
WHO WILL See You
THROUGH THE STORM

THE LORD KEEPS WATCH OVER YOU
AS YOU COME AND GO,
BOTH NOW AND FOREVER. PSALM 121:8

KEEP
CALM
AND
SHINE
ON!

LIVE
BY FAITH

-------- FOLDING LINE ——— CUTTING LINE

Cards TO COLOUR, CUT & FOLD

May God
bless you
and keep you.
Numbers 6:24

Blessings!

Faith.
Hope.
Love.

I ALWAYS THANK
MY GOD FOR YOU.
1 CORINTHIANS 1:4

THINKING
OF YOU

FOLDING LINE

FOLDING LINE

—— CUTTING LINE